1981

THE POETRY OF E. A. ROBINSON

EDWIN ARLINGTON ROBINSON

THE POETRY OF
EDWIN ARLINGTON ROBINSON

An Essay in Appreciation

BY

LLOYD MORRIS

WITH A BIBLIOGRAPHY BY
W. VAN R. WHITALL

Select Bibliographies Reprint Series

BOOKS FOR LIBRARIES PRESS
FREEPORT, NEW YORK

First Published 1923
Reprinted 1969

STANDARD BOOK NUMBER:
8369-5093-3

LIBRARY OF CONGRESS CATALOG CARD NUMBER:
70-99664

PRINTED IN THE UNITED STATES OF AMERICA

TO

E. M. M.

ACKNOWLEDGMENT

For the privilege of quoting from Mr. Robinson's poems, the author is indebted to the courtesy of The Macmillan Company, Charles Scribner's Sons, and Thomas Seltzer, Inc., the publishers of the various volumes of Mr. Robinson's work, a complete list of which will be found in the Bibliography.

All quotations have been made from the poems as printed in the *Collected Poems* (The Macmillan Company, 1921), with the single exception of two verses of "The Children of the Night," a poem not included in that volume, and which is quoted from *The Children of the Night*, published by Charles Scribner's Sons.

The author wishes likewise to record his very great obligation to Mr. W. Van R. Whitall, who with painstaking care prepared the excellent bibliography of Mr. Robinson's works included in this book.

CONTENTS

I: MEN

I

MEN

Of all contemporary American poets none has discovered to us, as lovers of poetry, a larger measure of poetic experience than Edwin Arlington Robinson; nor does the art of any make a more imperious demand upon our normal, but sometimes unconscious capacity for experiencing life poetically. Few poets have reflected more completely a life distinctively that of our country and our time or have more deeply shared in the ideas and the emotions by which our time has been affected. But it is likewise true that no American poet writing in our time has been more consistently preoccupied by those unchanging moods through which the spirit has revealed itself to every age.

The most compelling, if also the most immediately apparent quality of Mr. Robinson's poetry is its invariable dramatic power. To illuminate the present moment by revealing it as an inescapable reaping of the totality of a past has always been the core of his poetic method. This insight into life, this special way of apprehending experience constitutes one of the few explicit personal statements that his art affords. It conditions the intellectual content of his poetry, a con-

13

tent particularly significant because he has given us
not only a record, but a reading of life. And it is
freighted with additional importance to our understanding of his art, since it is only by the increasing
comprehensiveness of statement in which this special
insight has found expression that we may measure Mr.
Robinson's development as a creative artist.

That development itself has been somewhat unusual, for although it has resulted in an art more
widely extended in i^ts field of vision, it has not been
the consequence of any incremental subtlety of pene-
tration into human character, nor of any perfection of
technical mastery. I do not mean by this to imply
that Mr. Robinson has not gained in both depth and
power, as every serious artist must, with the maturity
of the passing years. But the quality of his insight,
the vivid characterisation, the haunting, inevitable
phrase which distinguish his poetry are as evident in
certain of the poems of his first book as they are in
certain others first published twenty-five years later
in the *Collected Poems*. The difference, for example,
between two such volumes as *The Children of the
Night* and *Merlin* is not mainly one of qualitative excellence. It is the difference between an art which
reveals humanity in the individual, psychologically
complete and sharply differentiated from his fellows,
and an art which reveals humanity in its eternal and
universal aspects, expressing those moods and aspirations which men, everywhere, have profoundly shared.
It is, in short, the difference between our romantic
western art, insistently concerned with the unique
values of the individual personality, and art like that

14

E. A. ROBINSON

of the Greeks or the Chinese, in which race ideas and race memory have fixed the serious interpretations of life of a people, and in which expression, drawing upon them, tends to conventionalise the pattern of life in a traditional symbolism. This development records a changing artistic intention with relation to which Mr. Robinson's purely dramatic poems seem to divide into three groups without any definite reference to the incidence of time. The portraits of contemporary figures constitute the first of these groups, the historical portraits the second, "Merlin" and "Lancelot" the third.

It was with the publication, in 1897, of *The Children of the Night*—rather than that of *The Torrent and the Night Before,* a slim book privately printed in the previous year which is now one of the most eagerly sought of modern first editions—that readers of poetry became acquainted with the earliest of a series of portraits of "Tilbury Town" folk to which Mr. Robinson has added at intervals ever since. We need but recall the influences under which American poets were then writing, as has lately been pointed out by a discriminating critic,[1] to realise how greatly Mr. Robinson was an innovator of the spirit, and how extensive has been the effect of his art upon a whole generation of American poets. To dispraise the art of that period, possibly without quite knowing why, is now a fashionable critical attitude. Certainly its chief preoccupation could hardly be more alien to our interests. There had been a valiant attempt to trans-

[1] Herbert S. Gorman in *The New Republic,* February 8, 1922.

15

243

plant the pallid energies of the "decadence," and for a brief period the influence of the *Yellow Book* flourished in the windy atmosphere of Chicago. There was, too, the equally brief vogue of vers de société, during which a respectable number of versifiers wrote pleasant and occasionally charming imitations of Austin Dobson's lyrics. There were the *Songs from Vagabondia* which established a well-bred convention of unconventionality. And there were the older generation, Gilder, Aldrich and a group of figures less distinguished.

Our current impatience with the verse of the period may be attributed to the fact that, however rich in grace—and much of it was graceful—it wholly fails to touch us emotionally or intellectually. The best poets of the period were writing about subjects perfectly natural to them in a way equally natural; neither the content nor the manner are natural to us. If this should seem a somewhat cavalier treatment of reputations not yet wholly forgotten, we may console ourselves by remembering that similar cleavages in the past have usually worked out to the very great advantage of poetry. For Mr. Robinson, who was then in his twenties, to have been greatly influenced by the literary preoccupations of the time would not have been unusual. But they seem to have hardly affected him in any tangible way except in a single instance. This exception was the almost exclusive interest which poets were then taking in poetic form and in the cultivation, within a limited range, of technical perfection. Mr. Robinson shared this interest, as a reference to *The Torrent and The Night Before*

and *The Children of the Night* reveals, and it con-
tributed to his poetic equipment a mastery of expression which is one of the most characteristic elements
of his art. But his early experiments in the various
lyric forms indicate very clearly his essentially dramatic gift, his capacity for projecting a situation or
a story through a mood. Compare, for example,
Austin Dobson's use of the fragile and delicate villa-
nelle in the familiar

> "When I saw you last, Rose,
>   You were only so high;—
> How fast the time goes!
>
> Like a bud ere it blows,
>   You just peeped at the sky,
> When I saw you last, Rose!"

with Mr. Robinson's evocation of a sombre mood and
an unrevealed tragedy in "The House on the Hill," in
which he employs the same lyric form:

> "They are all gone away,
>   The House is shut and still,
> There is nothing more to say.
>
> Through broken walls and gray
>   The winds blow bleak and shrill:
> They are all gone away.
>
> Nor is there one to-day
>   To speak them good or ill:
> There is nothing more to say.

THE POETRY OF

Why is it then we stray
　Around the sunken sill?
They are all gone away,

And our poor fancy-play
　For them is wasted skill:
There is nothing more to say.

There is ruin and decay
　In the House on the Hill
They are all gone away,
There is nothing more to say."

    The portraits of the "Tilbury Town" figures included in *The Children of the Night* mark very definitely a break with poetic tradition and the beginning of an adventure of discovery. If the poetry of the period seems to have lacked any very vital relation to life, and to have been rather lamely subservient to a code of supposedly "literary" conventions, a similar charge can hardly be brought against the work of the novelists. The theory of realism, long preached and to some extent practised by Howells, that literature is the expression of life and is to be judged only by its fidelity to life, was beginning to bear fruit in the work of Hamlin Garland, Paul Leicester Ford, Stephen Crane, Margaret Deland and others. These writers, either implicitly in their art, or explicitly in their critical writing, were asserting as a privilege and a responsibility the liberty of the novelist to deal frankly and truthfully with any phase of the life about him; and to deal with it in its own terms. It is difficult to conceive that what now seems so elementary and orthodox an artistic position

18

E. A. ROBINSON

should have been seriously questioned, but it is important to remember that the doctrines of realism and naturalism were then being attacked not from the point of view of their effectiveness as literary methods, but, with an astonishing lack of sophistication, from the point of view of their validity. In the meanwhile, during the course of this energetic battle of the books, the poets retired from the scene of debate, and with a single exception, were unconcerned with the new liberty. That one exception was Mr. Robinson, who announced no programme and published no opinions. He did, however, something of far greater value to literature. He brought out a volume of verse which demonstrated conclusively that there is no such thing as an "unpoetic" subject, and which was the first to bring into the field of poetry the content and the method of the realistic novel.

In the discovery of the content and the method of realistic art there is nothing inherently unusual. Looking backward over literature it probably occurs to us that the discovery is one which each generation makes for itself. And in our own day, certainly as regards our novelists, the recurrent truth that the innovators of one generation are the academicians of the next has been demonstrated with almost devastating irony. With poetry, however, the situation has been somewhat different. The elements which Mr. Robinson imported into our poetry may be very simply described. They were, in the first place, a disposition to find in the common experience of American life the subject matter of poetry, and, secondly, a desire to express that experience directly and naturally. Natu-

19

ral expression did not mean obvious expression to Mr.
Robinson, as it has to certain of his contemporaries;
it meant obtaining in the rhythm of verse the effect of
the rhythms of common speech, and preserving in its
diction the sequence of the spoken word. It seems
hardly an exaggeration to say of Mr. Robinson that
he shared Wordsworth's desire to write with his eye on
the object, and that, like Wordsworth, he would have
the poet's utterance formed by the cadence of natural
speech. The effect of his innovations in content and
method upon the subsequent course of American poetry
have been far-reaching. To attribute to Mr. Robinson
direct responsibility for the "new poetry" would not
be, I think, wholly to his taste. But the fact remains
that Mr. Robinson himself was the first of the "new"
poets, and unquestionably the force of his ideals has
profoundly influenced the writing of such later ar-
rivals as, for example, Mr. Frost and Mr. Masters.

Mr. Robinson's insight is dramatic; he is concerned
chiefly with personality and the dynamics of human
character, especially with character in those moments
of choice in which a complete past is harvested;
his method, as we have seen, is founded on that of
prose realism. The results of this very individual collaboration are apparent in the long series of dramatic
portraits of Tilbury Town characters, each distinctive,
each sharply and mordantly etched. These poems
have a flavour of tonic irony, at times of disillusion,
in which many critics profess to have found Mr. Robinson's commentary on life; but this slightly astringent
quality, as a moment's reflection might indicate, is an
effect of the fusion of insight and method peculiar to

E. A. ROBINSON

the poet, and an apparent simplicity of poetic technique. The dramatist sets in operation a chain of cir-
cumstances in which his characters are unconsciously
brought to book by their own past. The method of the
naturalistic novelist is quite different; absolved of the
necessity of a demonstration, he tends to be less and
less concerned with incident and to become preoccupied with the effect of experience on character; the
drama is purely internal and is revealed by minute
and acute psychological analysis. When this method
is applied to dramatic material the very absence of the
terms in the demonstration essential to the dramatist
produces the effect of irony. Consider, for example,
Richard Cory:

"Whenever Richard Cory went down town,
  We people on the pavement looked at him:
  He was a gentleman from sole to crown,
  Clean favoured, and imperially slim.

And he was always quietly arrayed,
  And he was always human when he talked;
  But still he fluttered pulses when he said,
  'Good morning,' and he glittered when he walked.

And he was rich—yes, richer than a king—
  And admirably schooled in every grace:
  In fine, we thought that he was everything
  To make us wish that we were in his place.

So on we worked, and waited for the light,
  And went without the meat, and cursed the bread;
  And Richard Cory, one calm summer night,
  Went home and put a bullet through his head."

Here we have a man's life-story distilled into sixteen lines. A dramatist would have been under the necessity of justifying the suicide by some train of events in which Richard Cory's character would have inevitably betrayed him. A novelist would have dissected the psychological effects of these events upon Richard Cory. The poet, with a more profound grasp of life than either, shows us only what life itself would show us; we know Richard Cory only through the effect of his personality upon those who were familiar with him, and we take both the character and the motive for granted as equally inevitable. Therein lies the ironic touch, which is intensified by the simplicity of the poetic form in which this tragedy is given expression.

In all of Mr. Robinson's dramatic poems, whether they be the brief dramatic portraits like "Richard Cory," "Reuben Bright," "Cliff Klingenhagen," or "Aaron Stark," the miser who had "eyes like little dollars in the dark," or such longer poems as "Isaac and Archibald," "Aunt Imogen" or "Captain Craig," there is a complete revelation of the individual life, and it is because of this capacity for the creation of character in three dimensions that criticism of his work is so largely concerned with ideas which traditionally have been more frequently applied to the work of the novelist or playwright than to that of the poet. There are certain remarkable qualities in these poems almost unique in our literature with Mr. Robinson, and of these one of the most important is their penetrating diagnosis of complex psychological states. He has something of

E. A. ROBINSON

the Greek attitude in feeling that the essential drama
of life lies in the inward effect of experience upon the
spirit, and that action is important only in so far as
it provides a release back into the external world of
those forces which it has generated. In an art founded
upon this conception, the service of external action
to the beholder is not that of illuminating ideal values,
but of illustrating practical conclusions, and with these
the artist is not at all concerned. Thus, in a wholly
pure form, such an art would reflect experience only
in its spiritual consequences by revealing the behaviour
of the emotions and the intellect under the influence
of the external world, but the stimulus and the dis-
charge, being obvious, would tend also to be negligible.
It may be observed that this type of art, in so far as
it is concerned with character, demands a completely
objective method, and one necessarily analytic and intellectual. For this concentrated, intellective analysis
of the processes of the heart and mind of his characters Mr. Robinson possesses an aptitude which frequently seems sheer genius. It is because he con-
ceives experience in this way, that in so many of his
purely dramatic poems the external story seems never
to be written; the "elliptical method" which many of
his critics have remarked is merely his way of ap-
proaching experience with the greatest directness, of
shedding a brilliant light on what he feels to be fundamentally important, and relegating the obvious incident to implication. Vincent d'Indy some years ago
illustrated the method in music in his lovely *Istar,* a
series of variations on a theme which itself is never
heard though it dominates the composition. Many of

23

Mr. Robinson's poems exercise a similarly tantalising magic upon our imagination.

Because this magic is one of the most distinctive qualities of his writing, I quote several of those poems which to me seem singularly to emphasise it. "Fleming Helphenstine" is one of the simplest illustrations:

"At first I thought there was a superfine
  Persuasion in his face; but the free glow
  That filled it when he stopped and cried 'Hollo!'
Shone joyously, and so I let it shine.
He said his name was Fleming Helphenstine,
  But be that as it may;—I only know
  He talked of this and that and So-and-So
And laughed and chaffed like any friend of mine.

But soon, with a queer, quick frown, he looked at me,
  And I looked hard at him; and there we gazed
In a strained way that made us cringe and wince:
Then, with a wordless clogged apology
  That sounded half confused and half amazed,
He dodged,—and I have never seen him since."

In "Eros Turannos" he gives us the node of a human relationship which has terminated in failure:

"She fears him, and will always ask
    What fated her to choose him;
She meets in his engaging mask
    All reasons to refuse him;
But what she meets and what she fears
Are less than are the downward years,
Drawn slowly to the foamless weirs
    Of age, were she to lose him.

24

E. A. ROBINSON

Between a blurred sagacity
  That once had power to sound him,
And Love, that will not let him be
  The Judas that she found him,
Her pride assuages her almost,
As if it were alone the cost.—
He sees that he will not be lost
  And waits and looks around him.

A sense of ocean and old trees
  Envelops and allures him;
Tradition, touching all he sees,
  Beguiles and reassures him;
And all her doubts of what he says
Are dimmed with what she knows of days—
Till even prejudice delays
  And fades, and she secures him.

The falling leaf inaugurates
  The reign of her confusion;
The pounding wave reverberates
  The dirge of her illusion;
And home, where passion lived and died,
Becomes a place where she can hide,
While all the town and harbor side
  Vibrate with her seclusion.

We tell you, tapping on our brows,
  The story as it should be,—
As if the story of a house
  Were told, or ever could be;
We'll have no kindly veil between
Her visions and those we have seen,—
As if we guessed what hers have been,
  Or what they are or would be.

25

Meanwhile we do no harm; for they
   That with a god have striven,
Not hearing much of what we say,
   Take what the god has given;
Though like waves breaking it may be,
Or like a changed familiar tree,
Or like a stairway to the sea
   Where down the blind are driven."

There is here the whole story and no story at all; but with a fine intuitive understanding the poet has put before us all that is really essential, the effect on two people of a complete experience, and their relation to each other.   This method of expressing life has occasionally led Mr. Robinson to so thoroughly suppress what he feels to be the obvious as to wholly baffle the reader; an instance of this is to be found in "The Whip," a poem in which, as in d'Indy's *Istar*, the major theme does not make its appearance:

   "The doubt you fought so long
    The cynic net you cast,
    The tyranny, the wrong,
    The ruin, they are past;
    And here you are at last,
    Your blood no longer vexed;
    The coffin has you fast,
    The clod will have you next.

    But fear you not the clod,
    Nor ever doubt the grave:
    The roses and the sod
    Will not forswear the wave.

E. A. ROBINSON

The gift the river gave
Is now but theirs to cover:
The mistress and the slave
Are gone now, and the lover.

You left the two to find
Their own way to the brink
Then—shall I call you blind?—
You chose to plunge and sink.
God knows the gall we drink
Is not the mead we cry for,
Nor was it, I should think—
For you—a thing to die for.

Could we have done the same,
Had we been in your place?—
This funeral of your name
Throws no light on the case.
Could we have made the chase,
And felt then as you felt?—
But what's this on your face,
Blue, curious, like a welt?

There were some ropes of sand
Recorded long ago,
But none, I understand,
Of water. Is it so?
And she—she struck the blow,
You but a neck behind. . . .
You saw the river flow—
Still, shall I call you blind?"

Another point with regard to Mr. Robinson's long
gallery of portraits of individuals is peculiarly noteworthy. All of the characters whose lives he has por-

27

trayed are in some way, if only at a single moment, unaccommodated to the world of experience. Flammonde can disentangle the skein of other people's lives, but is himself withheld from "the destinies that came so near to being his." Old King Cole, despite his urbanity, finds no balm for his grief over his "two disastrous heirs." Briony and Tasker Norcross are alike defeated by a destiny within them in the very fulness of their affluence. Llewellyn, driven to escape from his termagant wife Priscilla, has one brief moment of victory; but that "skirt-crazed reprobate," John Evereldown, has none. Reuben Bright, the butcher, bewails the death of his wife and tears down the slaughter house. Aunt Imogen finds her moment of happiness exquisite in its very anguish. Captain Craig, the least favoured by fortune, has learned "to laugh with God" and is protected from failure by the humour which he has distilled from disillusion. And who can forget the ironic beauty with which Mr. Robinson has portrayed Isaac and Archibald, two gentle old men, each of them dreading the incapacity of age, and each, in his anxiety to disclaim its incidence, seeing its descent upon the other? All of these figures, and twice as many more, proclaim the poet's abiding sympathy for those who, unable to control experience, are swept by it into defeat. It is not quite defeat if there still remain courage and the will to live fully; that is what many feel to be Mr. Robinson's intuition of "success in failure":

"Though the sick beast infect us, we are fraught
Forever with indissoluble Truth,

E. A. ROBINSON

Wherein redress reveals itself divine,
Transitional, transcendent. Grief and loss,
Disease and desolation, are the dreams
Of wasted excellence; and every dream
Has in it something of an ageless fact
That flouts deformity and laughs at years."

This apprehension of a way of reconciliation of the disharmony of experience has a somewhat special bearing in relation to Mr. Robinson's philosophical ideas, and we may best defer consideration of it to the discussion of those ideas; for the moment it is sufficient to observe the frequent emphasis which it has found in the dramatic portraits.

In no one of Mr. Robinson's poems has his capacity for probing into the hidden recesses of the spirit been more clearly demonstrated than in the revised version of that long poem, "Avon's Harvest," to which he refers as his "dime novel." Of all the external stories implied by his dramatic poems, this is the most carefully and sensitively articulated and the most completely revealed. In fact, the sheer dexterity with which Mr. Robinson has built up situation is likely to obscure the less immediately apparent, but more finely artistic excellence of the poem. In the first published version of the poem there were certain flaws which dissatisfied Mr. Robinson, and it is a rewritten and perfected version which appears in the *Collected Poems*. As it now stands, "Avon's Harvest" is a powerful and haunting analysis of the effects upon the mind and spirit of hate and fear. We noted before that external action seems of little importance in Mr. Robinson's art, and that he is chiefly concerned with the modifica-

29

tion of the spirit by experience. In "Avon's Harvest"
he shows the necessity which life imposes upon the individual to release into the external world the spiritual
forces which experience kindles in the mind and the
emotions. The tragedy of Avon is that of a man who
is unable to accomplish this release, and who is killed
by the consuming energy of the hatred and the fear
which, constantly repressed, motivate his entire life.
In this poem Mr. Robinson has conveyed the complete
spiritual biography of a character by means of an almost lapidary reproduction of the shifting moods and
feelings which accompany the gradually crescent moral
disintegration. As one more illustration of that curious cerebral magic which Mr. Robinson frequently
exercises, I quote a passage from "Avon's Harvest" de-
scribing the genesis of fear:

> " 'It was not anything my eyes had seen
> That I could feel around me in the night,
> There by that lake. If I had been alone,
> There would have been the joy of being free,
> Which in imagination I had won
> With unimaginable expiation—
> But I was not alone. If you had seen me,
> Waiting there for the dark and looking off
> Over the gloom of that relentless water,
> Which had the stillness of the end of things
> That evening on it, I might well have made
> For you the picture of the last man left
> Where God, in his extinction of the rest,
> Had overlooked him and forgotten him.
> Yet I was not alone. Interminably
> The minutes crawled along and over me,

E. A. ROBINSON

Slow, cold, intangible, and invisible,
As if they had come up out of that water.
How long I sat there I shall never know,
For time was hidden out there in the black lake,
Which now I could see only as a glimpse
Of black light by the shore. There were no stars
To mention, and the moon was hours away
Behind me. There was nothing but myself
And what was coming. . . .' "

Over one more quality of Mr. Robinson's portraits
of individuals the memory willingly lingers. And that
is the exquisite humour, so very characteristic of the
man personally, which runs through them like a silver
thread. It ranges from a tender, almost wistful mock-
ery to edged and scintillant satire, and it plays fitfully
over the whole long gallery of characters. In such a
poem as "Isaac and Archibald" the humour is like the
touch of a cool hand; in the variations of Greek
themes it breaks into rippling laughter; in "Theophi-
lus" as in "Momus" and several others there is the
finely sensitive twist of a scalpel. In "Captain Craig"
Mr. Robinson has given us not only a poem, but a
philosophy of which humour is the essence; the humour here is cerebral and concentrated, a bulwark to
the sea of fate. But to me the most characteristic
example of the flavour of his humour, and for that
reason one of the most notable of his poems, is "Miniver Cheevy":

"Miniver Cheevy, child of scorn,
    Grew lean while he assailed the seasons;
He wept that he was ever born,
    And he had reasons.

31

E. A. ROBINSON

Miniver loved the days of old
   When swords were bright and steeds were
      prancing;
The vision of a warrior bold
   Would set him dancing.

Miniver sighed for what was not,
   And dreamed, and rested from his labors;
He dreamed of Thebes and Camelot,
   And Priam's neighbors.

Miniver mourned the ripe renown
   That made so many a name so fragrant;
He mourned Romance now on the town,
   And Art, a vagrant.

Miniver loved the Medici,
   Albeit he had never seen one;
He would have sinned incessantly
   Could he have been one.

Miniver cursed the commonplace
   And eyed a khaki suit with loathing;
He missed the mediæval grace
   Of iron clothing.

Miniver scorned the gold he sought
   But sore annoyed was he without it;
Miniver thought, and thought, and thought,
   And thought about it.

Miniver Cheevy, born too late,
   Scratched his head and kept on thinking;
Miniver coughed, and called it fate,
   And kept on drinking."

II: HISTORY

II

HISTORY

Mr. Woodberry, in *A New Defence of Poetry*, contrasts with extraordinary lucidity the divergent and opposed tendencies in art to which custom has given the names of realism and idealism. The fundamental opposition, he tells us, lies in the subject of interest. Are we concerned chiefly with knowing others as different from ourselves? Then we choose an art specially interpretative of the individual. Do we wish to know ourselves in others? Then our art must be widely interpretative of the common nature of men.

The definition of this contrast must inevitably suggest itself to the reader of Mr. Robinson's poetry who passes from his dramatic portraits of individual personalities—the Tilbury figures and the others—to that splendid group of poems in which he has revived a series of historical figures: Lincoln, Napoleon, Shakespeare, Rembrandt, Paul, Lazarus, John Brown, Burr and Hamilton. It was, perhaps, the probing, searching temper of Mr. Robinson's mind, his abiding interest in the springs of character and personality, which led him from minute analysis of the individual to a first tentative synthesis. In the historical poems his imagination has been stirred by character, by personality, by the drama of individual life, but in a special sense.

His interest here is in those figures which the memory of the race has carried into history because each of them has quintessentially embodied some eternal mood or aspiration of the human spirit. I do not know whether Mr. Robinson has, like Carlyle, any theory regarding heroes. But if he has, I conceive it as being unlike Carlyle's; great men seem quite simply to him to be the expression of normal humanity in an exalted moment. The very nature of his selection of figures tells us much. For as history records them, the drama of these men's lives centred in a spiritual conflict between the lyric insight of the ideal, and the reprobation of a practical world, which had no vision. Sometimes, as in the case of Shakespeare, the world and the ideal are the dualities of the individual soul. With Paul the conflict is between two ideals. Lincoln, Rembrandt and John Brown project the conflict into the world of men. The tragedy of Lazarus, beautifully conceived, is that of a spirit made free of two worlds, but at home in neither.

Over many readers of Mr. Robinson's poetry this series of portraits of historical characters will exercise with an added intensity the familiar magic peculiar to the briefer portraits of individuals. The emotion of recognition is not without special advantages as a channel of appeal, and a poet who draws on history for his subjects faces an audience already disciplined by a common culture and tradition. It is perhaps because such preparation produces a more active collaboration of the audience with the poet that these historical poems appeal to us primarily as noble interpretations of the specific spirit of individual men.

E. A. ROBINSON

What poet has more persuasively revived the rounded humanity of Shakespeare or more exactly phrased his practical ambitions, his visions of life, his naïvely speculative spirit? And is there not, by way of contrast, a brilliant study of Ben Jonson, scholar and cynic, artist and man of humour? Recall the simplicity and the rugged nobility of Mr. Robinson's Lincoln, whose character is revealed, through a method of which Mr. Robinson has made frequent use, in the effect of Lincoln upon other men. We may well admire an intuitive tact which recognised that Ben Jonson's discourse of Shakespeare, and the estimate of Lincoln by opponents who were unwillingly swept under the banner of his fame interpret Shakespeare and Lincoln with greater poetic truth by reason of their very indirection. To appreciate the rightness of this choice we have but to consider how unwillingly we should listen to a poet who would have Shakespeare or Lincoln soliloquise, and how inevitably far short such talk would fall of what the memory of the race imagines it. The monologue of Napoleon at St. Helena does not arouse this special criticism of the imagination, since the petulance and the fevered complaint of its tone provokes the particular emotional response which is its purpose. And again, recalling the account which Paul has given of his own philosophy, what more dramatic and natural moment could the poet have chosen for its interpretation than that of Paul's meeting with the brethren at The Three Taverns on his journey to Rome?

Unquestionably these poems evoke our admiration as subtly interpretative analyses of individual charac-

ters. They make clear that fine capacity for compre-
hension and sympathy which is one of the most distinctively personal attributes of all Mr. Robinson's
works. They demonstrate, on a somewhat larger can-
vas than the Tilbury portraits, Mr. Robinson's per-
spicacity into human nature, and his unique ability,
among all contemporary American poets, in the condensed dramatic summation of a spiritual biography.
But they are even more important in the final account
of his work up to the present since they represent
his first extended generalisations about life, and—as
we shall see in due course—Mr. Robinson has given a
singularly noble, and to the modern mind, moving interpretation of life.

One of the doctrines which undoubtedly has
coloured much of Mr. Robinson's reflection on life
is that which the philosophers, in their professional
terminology, call idealism. Stripped of its various
critical implications, the position of the idealists has
very much in common with the philosophy of Emerson and the transcendental school. Briefly, their
theory is that all human beings are part of one infinite life, and that the ends of this Absolute are best
served through the cultivation by each individual of
his special aptitudes. It is not necessary here to show
the effect that this philosophic position has had upon
Mr. Robinson's theory of life; it is sufficient to point
out that adherence to the position logically entails
certain direct consequences. In the first place, it suggests the virtue of positive action, of individualism.
It likewise suggests the validity of individual insight
and thereby counsels a certain tolerance in our moral

E. A. ROBINSON

judgments. Finally it implies a certain ultimate poetic equality of value. It is easy to see why the method of realistic art, concerned primarily with individual experience and abstaining too delicate an eclecticism as between experiences, should inevitably appeal to a poet who was intellectually attracted to the theory of idealism. But the artist and the thinker usually discover a fundamental limitation in the method. If humanity shares in common a small stake in the infinite, its recognition of that common possession is quite likely to be humanity's most significant gesture. The artist who makes an ideal of objective truth to individual experience must gradualiy come to feel that a record of observation is not enough; uninterpreted observation does not count among its contributions to knowledge a single working hypothesis. And if his art is to be relevant to eternal human experience it must in some way interpret what seems eternal in it.

The realist, however anxious he may be to give human life this ideal interpretation, is usually distrustful of ideal generalisations not firmly rooted in the objective reality of experience with which his art is chiefly concerned. Not for him is the romanticist's adventure of creating a world of the imagination with a method which may turn out to be one of the many that the Creator happened to reject! And so the realist's first generalisations of ideal values are likely to have a special reference to the past. Here he is on the sure ground of reality, but his interest in external reality is essentially in the ideal values which it tends to illustrate. And his interest in these ideal

39

values is conditioned by their pertinence to contemporary moral experience. If his insight into the aims and aspirations of other men in other ages is to have dramatic force, it must draw this power from its relevance to the emotional life of men and women of his own time. In this respect the poet seems to illustrate a process which all of us recognise in practice as our own. What we call historical memory is uniquely a species of poetic activity common to all of us, whereby we validate the ideals of private judgment through some discovery of their eternal application. Our own practice tends to confirm Santayana's statement that the function of history is to lend materials to politics and poetry, since these arts need to dominate the past, the better to dominate the present situation and the ideal one.

From this point of view Mr. Robinson's portraits of historical figures, notwithstanding their excellence as interpretations of the specific spirit of individual men, derive their poetic value less from their truth to this objective reality than from the fact that they are essentially adventures in identification. In them brooding reflection over the ideal values of experience and human destiny brings the weight of a greater imperativeness to bear upon the observation of human life. We have noticed that in each case they illustrate a conflict between ideals and reality, but our interest reveals a more abiding significance. They are portraits of idealists, but of idealists who chose the path of individualistic self-development, who found in allegiance to their own insight an adequate way of life. It is, therefore, in their interpretation

E. A. ROBINSON

of some of the eternal ways in which the human mind
has met experience and sought to subject it to a
measure of control, that the best of these poems estab-
lish their communion with our spirit. For all men
share in some degree the poetic desire to refashion
life to their own satisfaction, and in the moods in
which this aspiration finds expression the cadence
of immortality seems most surely to dwell.

41

III: LEGEND

III

LEGEND

The fairest ideals and the most profound aspirations of the spirit draw their illustrations from historical memory; but the figures thus recorded are those which exemplify rather than formulate a people's serious interpretations of life. Such figures are memorable because they illuminate values eternally felt to be true, but for the expression of the ideal itself we go behind them to more spontaneous syntheses, those which have their first definition in legends and racial tradition, and their successive revaluations through time in art.

The very wealth of connotation and association which such legends have accreted through centuries of active collaboration not only of poets and artists, but of the popular mind as well, make them unusually complete records of spiritual experience, and hence every age finds it possible to cultivate a portion which seems especially relevant to its own problems and thus achieve a fresh interpretation. But if the fertility of legend in ideal associations and race ideas makes it a peculiarly subtle instrument of artistic expression, the paucity of its contacts with the criteria of external reality adds to its imaginative force. For the artist who finds in legend an appropriate language

45

is made free of a world which he may rebuild as he desires; we judge him not by his picture of reality, but by the power and significance of his ideals.

These two qualities of legend, its conventionalisation of the pattern of life into a traditional symbolism and its infinite variety of emotional overtones, are probably the secret of the attraction which it appears to exercise upon the minds of contemporary writers. A whole body of literature in Ireland has been created out of native folk-lore, and our American imagist poets, seeking to convey a finely condensed lyric impression, serve to remind us what our art owes to Oriental art, in which tradition has made the simplest attitude or gesture the symbol of an elaborate interpretation of experience. It is these two qualities which seem fundamentally contributive to the individual power of Mr. Robinson's "Merlin" and "Lancelot."

It betrays something more than casual misapprehension to consider these poems, as not a few critics have, merely attempts to retell the Arthurian legend. For obviously they are the result of a very different artistic intention. They represent, it seems to me, the distillation and the synthesis of a rigorous observation of human character and experience in terms of what the poet has come to believe is their most abiding and universal significance. In these poems the purely casual accidents of experience have been chiselled away; what remains is a dramatic reading of life as a career. In them the poet is concerned not with specific character, but with the eternal types of men and women; not with the unique effects of ex-

E. A. ROBINSON

perience upon the individual spirit, but with the
epical nobility of human destiny; not with the meticu-
lous analysis of mood, but with the high enterprise
of humanity in seeking dominion over an infinite universe through a finite and fragmentary wisdom. They
are an expression, and a singularly modern expression, of the perpetually recurrent moods of the human
spirit in its gesture toward immortality, of the enduring aspirations to beauty, to knowledge, to free-
dom, through which it seeks to resolve the final meaning of life.

Both "Merlin" and "Lancelot" were written under
the influence of the War and they are therefore necessarily pictures of a world in solution. There is a new
and strange beauty, tragic in its very opulence, in
their presentation of the collapse of a civilisation, of
the chaotic disintegration of its ideals, of the dawn
on far horizons of a new order imperfectly foreshad-
owed. They phrase with a brooding intensity the
emotions in which a disciplined faith found its first
response to the crashing impact of the War; a poign-
ant regret at the inevitable passing of beauty; a pa-
thetic acknowledgement of the failure of human rela-
tionships, a profound conviction of the ultimate
efficacy of moral idealism. There is, especially in
"Merlin," an exceedingly modern reading of events.
The War confronted us with the breakdown of intelligence as an instrument wherewith man might
control experience. This aspect of the situation is
reflected by the poet in Merlin's forlorn inability to
bring any power to bear upon the doom overhanging
Camelot. The symbolism in this instance should, one

47

imagines, be sufficiently apparent, and yet no less discerning a reader of poetry than Miss Amy Lowell seems to have missed, in her discussion of "Merlin," [1] one of its most significant ideas. Certainly the mood is clearly revealed in those lines in which the poet gives us the effect upon Arthur of his disastrous interview with Merlin and his realisation that even in Merlin's vision there is no further insight:

> "No tide that ever crashed on Lyonnesse
> Drove echoes inland that were lonelier
> For widowed ears among the fisher-folk,
> Than for the King were memories to-night
> Of old illusions that were dead forever."

But if the War seemed to illustrate the collapse of intelligence, it served to turn men's minds inward in a discovery of faith. This loyalty to an ideal revelation of the meaning of life is the integrating philosophy of all of Mr. Robinson's work, and in both "Merlin" and "Lancelot" it is the dominant dramatic motive. Nowhere in his poetry is there a more explicit illumination of that subtle concentration of experience into its ideal values than in these two poems, in which experience has its roots in passion and its meaning in a consecration of the spirit.

The completeness of this picture of life is what contributes to "Merlin" and "Lancelot" their superbly effective dramatic appeal. For the mind only reluctantly and not for long accepts an incomplete record of what its own vitality demonstrates to be a complete expe-

[1] "Tendencies in Modern American Poetry," pp. 67-68.

rience. Living, and not observation of life is the de-
terminant which scales our judgment of the validity
of any art, and itself makes us intuitively aware of
the truth which Santayana phrased in saying that
human reason lives by turning the friction of material forces into the light of ideal goods, and that all
life is animal in its origin and spiritual in its possible fruits. It is because these poems reveal life both
in its natural basis and in its spiritual ends, giving us
a reading of it as a total career, that they satisfy
equally our sense of its reality and our conviction of
its significance. The special insight which informs
them as expressions of complete experience is beautifully conveyed in Merlin's colloquy with Dagonet
just before their final departure from Camelot:

> " '. . . All this that was to be
> Might show to man how vain it were to wreck
> The world for self if it were all in vain.
> When I began with Arthur I could see
> In each bewildered man who dots the earth
> A moment with his days a groping thought
> Of an eternal will, strangely endowed
> With merciful illusions whereby self
> Becomes the will itself and each man swells
> In fond accordance with his agency.
> Now Arthur, Modred, Lancelot and Gawaine
> Are swollen thoughts of this eternal will
> Which have no other way to find the way
> That leads them on to their inheritance
> Than by the time-infuriating flame
> Of a wrecked empire, lighted by the torch
> Of woman, who, together with the light
> That Galahad found, is yet to light the world.' "

There is another aspect of both "Merlin" and "Lancelot" which merits the reader's attention. In the poems which we have previously considered experience and the interaction of personalities are reflected in so far as they impinge upon the consciousness of a single character; the drama converges entirely within that character's mind and emotions. But in the Arthurian poems the interplay of motive is more abundantly personalised, the range of character extended; the poet's imagination is preoccupied not by a revelation of the effects of life, but by a recreation of life itself. Furthermore, they are essentially love stories; not, it will be noted, pictures of the first flowering of youthful love, but of the heady and more fluent passion of maturity. Guinevere and Vivian are magnificently eloquent studies of women in love, and of the tragedy of love. Vivian, especially, has a quality of infinite pathos; her tragedy is that of a woman balked in her emotional potentialities, groping through love toward a more firmly integrated life. In Vivian there seems to be expressed all of that dawning self-consciousness, that curious and impressive search for fulfilment and for evaluation which characterise the contemporary feminine spirit. We think of her always as one

> ". . . whose unquiet heart is hungry
> For what is not, and what shall never be
> Without her, in a world that men are making,
> Knowing not how, nor caring yet to know
> How slowly and how grievously they do it,—"

and it is not without irony that reflection raises the

question that if the vision of Merlin or Lancelot be veritable, and therefore an imperative motive of life, should not the equally imperative intuition of Vivian and Guinevere, less facile but no less eager in its genesis, achieve the dignity of resolute expression? This, it would seem, is one of the implications which the poet has delicately insinuated into the very texture of his picture of life.

It is only when we think of "Merlin" and "Lancelot" as pictures of life having its roots in passion, that the mysterious glamour of sensuous beauty which they evoke is apparent. Few modern poets have given us a more chromatic orchestration of passion, or painted with more glowing palette the colours of romantic love. Recall, for example, this crescendo and its hushed coda, with its reflection of the climactic stress and subsidence of a mood:

". . . He bowed his head
And kissed the ten small fingers he was holding,
As calmly as if each had been a son;
Although his heart was leaping and his eyes
Had sight for nothing save a swimming crimson
Between two glimmering arms. 'More like a flower
To-night,' he said, as now he scanned again
The immemorial meaning of her face
And drew it nearer to his eyes. It seemed
A flower of wonder with a crimson stem
Came leaning slowly and regretfully
To meet his will—a flower of change and peril
That had a clinging blossom of warm olive
Half stifled with a tyranny of black,
And held the wayward fragrance of a rose
Made woman by delirious alchemy.

She raised her face and yoked his willing neck
With half her weight; and with hot lips that left
The world with only one philosophy
For Merlin or for Anaxagoras
Called his to meet them and in one long hush
Of capture to surrender and make hers
The last of anything that might remain
Of what was now their beardless wizardry.
Then slowly she began to push herself
Away, and slowly Merlin let her go
As far from him as his outreaching hands
Could hold her fingers while his eyes had all
The beauty of the woodland and the world
Before him in the firelight, like a nymph
Of cities, or a queen a little weary
Of inland stillness and immortal trees."

Recall, too, the fragile modulation of Lancelot's vision
of Guinevere as he rides toward their last interview
in the convent at Almesbury:

". . . And there was no Camelot now—
Now that no Queen was there, all white and gold,
Under an oaktree with another sunlight
Sifting itself in silence on her glory
Through the dark leaves above her where she sat,
Smiling at what she feared, and fearing least
What most there was to fear. Ages ago
That must have been; for a king's world had faded
Since then, and a king with it. Ages ago,
And yesterday, surely it must have been
That he had held her moaning in the firelight
And heard the roaring down of that long rain,
As if to wash away the walls that held them
Then for that hour together. Ages ago,

E. A. ROBINSON

And always, it had been that he had seen her,
As now she was, floating along before him,
Too far to touch and too fair not to follow,
Even though to touch her were to die. . . ."

It is unquestionably in "Merlin" and in "Lancelot" that Mr. Robinson's dramatic art has received its finest and most comprehensive expression. About them play the overtones of traditional association of what the memory of the race has cherished of an antique loveliness and an eternal perfection; of the abiding aspiration of the spirit, flowering in sense, to embody the immaterial glory of its vision in the tangible beauty of the physical world. They are at once a synthesis and an abstraction of experience, an expression of those moods of the spirit which are most permanent and most enduring and through which the eternal rediscovery of ideal values is eternally made. The adventure of that discovery is their content, and in it the pattern of life and its rhythm are simply, but profoundly resolved.

IV: PLAYS

IV

PLAYS

Mr. Robinson's two prose plays, *Van Zorn*, published in 1914, and *The Porcupine*, published in the following year, hold for us that peculiar interest we have in all experiments through which the creative artist seeks a fresh channel. There is always, as Browning knew, a spontaneous vitality in the transfer of imagination from the medium of expression in which it has been disciplined into an unaccustomed art. It is the vitality rather than the success of the experiment that appeals to us, and we are held chiefly by the creative energy involved in the artist's

" Using nature that's an art to others,
  Not, this one time, art that's turned his nature."

This quality of freshness, the product of a tentative essay in an unfamiliar technique, is what Mr. Robinson's two plays disclose.

Both *Van Zorn* and *The Porcupine* likewise reveal many of the characteristic elements of Mr. Robinson's art. They illustrate, for example, his essential directness in dealing with reality, and their theatrical inarticulacy seems largely to be the result of his inability to preoccupy himself with the obvious. His dramatic interest, we have observed, is in the inward effect of experience upon character, and this tends to relegate the external story to pure implication. In *Van Zorn* this conception of experience entirely dominates the drama, and the real play takes place, not in the action which runs its course before us, but in the minds of the characters who find themselves in the relentless grasp of fate. The instrument of fate, and one might almost say its personification, is the mysterious *Van Zorn*, whose vivid sense of the agency of an unaccomplished destiny fixes the brooding and burdened atmosphere that intangibly surrounds and plays upon the events. To project this atmosphere through the background of a colloquial comedy of contemporary manners is something of a *tour de force*, to make it seem psychologically veritable, as Mr. Robinson has succeeded in doing, is a sure, though in his case perhaps an unimportant, indication of dramatic power. The difficulty to be found with *Van Zorn* is not, as has been suspected, that it is undramatic, but that as a play it is not in accord with the special conventions of the contemporary theatre.

The Porcupine, however, seems almost a deliberate attempt to satisfy those special conventions by writing entirely within them. The interest here is firmly and almost exclusively in situation rather than in character, and the play suffers through the suppression of the vigorous architectonics of human nature in which Mr. Robinson's creative imagination habitually works. The subordination of character to plot suggests a compromise with the mechanics of an unaccustomed technique and an effort to build an art

E. A. ROBINSON

from the outside inward. One of the most subtle
beauties of Mr. Robinson's poetry is its capacity for
concentrated illumination of the fundamentally important effects of any given experience upon the
spirit. This excellence is not revealed in *The Porcupine*, which deals rather with the concomitant accidents of an experience than with the experience
itself.

There is evident in both these plays, however, much
of Mr. Robinson's force as an innovator in our art.
They are definitely experiments, within the range of
the art of the theatre, in the application of a characteristic naturalism to the contemporary American
scene, and to the material of contemporary American
life. It might be said with some degree of truth that
they are attempts to recast in the forms and through
the medium of another art, the essential content and
intention of his earliest dramatic portraits. It is from
this point of view that they are valuable to the reader
of his poetry, and it is as attempts in this direction,
rather than as independent æsthetic creations, that
their value may most profitably be ascertained.

V: IDEAS

V

IDEAS

One of the most important aspects of Mr. Robinson's art is its reflection of contemporary intellectual experience. He is one of the very few poets of modern America who, in recognising that ideas are properly subjects to which the emotions as well as the intellect might respond, has restored to our poetic feeling something of its antique comprehensiveness. We do not look to poetry to furnish us with a philosophy ready made, to offer us a systematised theory of life; even when, in the past, it has done so, that service has not been its most abiding ministration. But poetry offers us an effect peculiarly its own, an excitement of the imagination and a liberation of the spirit, which may be the consequence of an idea but is hardly an idea or a system of thought in itself. Mr. Robinson's poetry offers us just such contacts as this; it brings us a record of response to intellectual experience probably unmatched in our poetry since the days of Emerson.

The character of that experience is in itself illuminating; its central preoccupation is a quest for certainty the progress of which finds its first terms in the title poem of *The Children of the Night* and its final and mature convictions in the title poem of *The*

63

THE POETRY OF

Man Against the Sky. In this quest the poet re-
capitulates the fundamental intellectual adventure of
the period in which he has written, an adventure de-
termined in part by our inheritance of the Puritan
tradition and in part also by the critical temper of
the modern mind. The Puritan theology stamped in-
delibly upon the New England mind the conviction
that somehow every life represented a fresh chance for
ultimate salvation; coupled with this individualism
was a predisposition to speculation concerning the
validity of our perceptions of experience and its ultimate significance. With the decline in intellectual
influence of the Puritan creed, the speculative tendency of its genius cast itself adrift first and tentatively
upon empirical philosophy, which it found deficient,
if not sterile, in spiritual nourishment, and then upon
the sea of German idealism, which, although it revived the native individualism of the Puritan genius,
did not humiliate its relations with Divinity. It
seems to have been these two characteristics of the
New England temperament which enabled Emerson
to import ideas from the infinite with much the same
facility as Salem merchants were wont to import teak
from China.

The doctrines of transcendentalism captured the
imagination of philosophic thinkers in America for
several generations; they attached a romantic importance to intuition and its expression, which attained
the dignity not only of a report upon the state of the
individual spirit, but of the complexities of an entire
universe. The essence of that doctrine was an affirma-
tion of the soul's capacity for perceiving the truth by

64

means of inspirational intuition frequently to be achieved in a species of mystical rapture. Here, of course, was the Puritan conception of religion as an individual, personal and inward experience; and to it was joined a conception of God as an oversoul, a single reality in which all existence is comprehended. From this conception proceeds the theory that the soul of the individual is identical with the soul of the universe, and that the individual's obligation in life is to detect, in those moments of vision and insight, his own potentialities, and then to set about resolutely cultivating their highest development. Finally, just as the individual is a part of the Absolute mind, the transcendentalists felt that nature is equally one of its aspects, a manifestation of spirit in a sensual world.

But although the speculations of the transcendentalists resulted in a number of theories about existence, they did not produce an integrated metaphysical system. Their idealistic philosophy was an attitude of mind and a way of apprehending life, but not a rationalised interpretation of the universe. The construction of a philosophical system upon the foundations of transcendentalism was left to a later romantic philosopher, Josiah Royce, who was something of a mystic, and was filled with the mystic's wistful yearning for final certitude. And, although we need not linger over Royce's system, two characteristic elements are noteworthy. His chief concern was to prove that all lives are parts of a unified and omniscient Absolute life which holds the key to the problem of existence. But whereas the transcendentalists were naïvely satisfied to dismiss error and evil as a king of negative virtue implicit in our finite wisdom, Royce felt the burdens of a complicated world in which both error and evil seemed to be predominant. It was, perhaps, the modern mind's criticism of pure faith which impelled him to prove the existence of the Absolute through the existence of error. And it was characteristic of his moralistic tendency to find in evil an expression of the will of a perfect and omnipotent Absolute; a kind of shadow against which the contrasting high light of virtue rejoiced the æsthetic sense of the Absolute.

It is easy to see why Royce's romantic idealism, compounded of the transcendental individualism inherited from the Puritan tradition and the old Calvinistic intuition of original sin, should have offered a consolation and a refuge to many troubled spirits beyond that of a traditional religion by which they were not very profoundly moved. And it is undoubtedly true that Royce's sincerity, his earnest faith, and his fierce enthusiasm for final certitude left an abiding impression upon several generations of men who were students at Harvard when he held a chair of philosophy in that university. Mr. Robinson, who was at Harvard during that period, reveals in his poems a very definite preoccupation with the implications of the metaphysics of idealism.

The difficulties of the followers of the idealistic philosophy are many, and though Royce, granting the truth of his postulates, seems to have resolved them with the greatest logical consistency from his own point of view, some of his disciples have found them-

selves temperamentally unable to follow him whole-
heartedly. The gravest of these difficulties are the
method of pure faith and intuition upon which the
whole structure of romantic idealism is predicated,
and at which intellectual scepticism is disposed to
cavil; and the justification of evil as the will of an
infinite and perfect Absolute. On the one hand the
question arises as to whether faith in intuitional revelation unsupported by scientific logic is not a cow-
ardly avoidance of the major issue. Or is it, in truth,
man's most profoundly intelligent expression? Is the
revelation, the "Light," itself veritable, or is it
merely an imaginative delusion whereby we effect a
compromise with hope? On the other hand, how is a
world so patently replete with evil, with injustice, and
with failure of ideals, to be reconciled with a beneficent
destiny of which we ourselves are a part? Or is this
world nothing more than a "blind atomic pilgrimage"
governed only by fortuitous causation? These are
the problems which have peculiarly beset the modern
mind, torn between its loyalties to faith and to science,
to a traditional religious optimism and the profoundly
pessimistic realities of experience. For many the
position is summed up in Lancelot's despairing cry:

" 'God, what a rain of ashes falls on him
    Who sees the new and cannot leave the old!' "

These are the ideas and the questions and the doubts
of which many of Mr. Robinson's poems are a record.
"The Children of the Night," which Mr. Robinson
has omitted from the *Collected Poems,* is the earliest

67

poem in which his reaction to these various problems
is set forth with any degree of fulness. It is a very simple statement of faith in a purposeful world, and of
belief in the power of the inner light. But it shows
the critical and analytical temper of Mr. Robinson's
mind that this faith, which to the transcendentalist
would derive its validity from the fact that it is a pure
intuition, is by him arrived at through the logic of a
negative argument. The first two verses state his
belief:

> "For those that never know the light,
>   The darkness is a sullen thing;
> And they, the Children of the Night,
>   Seem lost in Fortune's winnowing.

> But some are strong and some are weak,—
>   And there's the story. House and home
> Are shut from countless hearts that seek
>   World-refuge that will never come."

There are two aspects of a single idea in this poem
which recur as themes throughout almost the entire
range of Mr. Robinson's work; one is the notion of
the intuition of truth; the other, the "common creed
of common sense." The intuition of truth is the "light"
which somehow reveals itself to us in a world in which
the spirit is burdened by thwarted hopes and humili-
ated ideals. If the light comes, the poet suggests,
common sense counsels our acceptance of it on its own
terms; the fact that the world of our experience offers
neither warrant nor verification of its promise is the

E. A. ROBINSON

most powerful argument for its validity. The doctrine of self-reliance and individualism, the theory that each of us contains a spark of divinity, since we are all comprehended within the universal mind, is likewise expressed in "The Children of the Night." It is, as we have seen, one of the motivating ideas in all of Mr. Robinson's dramatic portraits and poems of character. Of all the characters that he has created only those who have no light to follow—such characters as Tasker Norcross or Richard Cory or Briony,—are really in his sense failures. His counsel is one of positive action and of positive acceptance; follow the light no matter where it may lead you; follow it in spite of the fact that the wisdom of material experience may believe you a fool, in so doing lies the way of wisdom and the way of virtue; develop your own potentialities to the fullest, no matter what they may be, for in so doing you are fulfilling your destiny. This is hardly a philosophy of quietism or of pessimism, and critics who have read such philosophies into Mr. Robinson's poetry seem simply to have misinterpreted a devotion to ideals so profoundly exclusive that it results in a supreme indifference to their material consequences. This attitude of mind is likewise the explanation, it seems to me, of what some of his critics have felt to be a doctrine of "success through failure." The failure which they see is, for Mr. Robinson at least, not failure; it is merely the realist's recognition of the ironic discord between material experience and spiritual ideals.

One of the finest statements of his intuitive and mystic philosophy which Mr. Robinson has given is

69

contained in a magnificent early sonnet, entitled "Credo":

"I cannot find my way: there is no star
In all the shrouded heavens anywhere;
And there is not a whisper in the air
Of any living voice but one so far
That I can hear it only as a bar
Of lost, imperial music, played when fair
And angel fingers wove, and unaware,
Dead leaves to garlands where no roses are.

No, there is not a glimmer, nor a call,
For one that welcomes, welcomes when he fears,
The black and awful chaos of the night;
For through it all—above, beyond it all—
I know the far-sent message of the years,
I feel the coming glory of the Light."

But the final, and the most eloquent statement of Mr. Robinson's theory of life is "The Man Against the Sky." This poem, which is one of the noble justifications in poetry of idealism, is likewise one of the few highly serious readings of life to be found in the whole field of American poetry. It reveals the profound vision and the beauty of utterance; the intellectual vigour and the emotional power; above all, the poetic insight and the spiritual liberation which have been the significant characteristics of Mr. Robinson's verse.

We have but to compare with the symphonic orchestration and the noble intellectual design of "The Man Against the Sky" the simplicity of "The Children of the Night" to become aware of the development and the extension of power which accrued during the inter-

70

E. A. ROBINSON

vening years. Whereas "The Children of the Night" is a declaration of personal faith, "The Man Against the Sky" is a poignantly imaginative vision of the whole of life, which marches relentlessly to a majestic conclusion. Into it has gone, by a species of spiritual metabolism, all the acute observation, all the brooding reflection over existence which produced the preceding poems. In it the authority of emotional faith and the integrity of intellectual conviction are fused into incandescence.

"The Man Against the Sky" has been termed a refutation of the mechanistic conception of the universe; it is so, but only incidentally. Rather it is a lucid and moving summation of the significant creeds with which men have sought to fortify their souls, of the chief ways in which the mind and spirit have oriented themselves with respect to the universe and attempted to impose their tenure upon it. It proceeds to its conclusion with a remarkable, and for many minds, an eternal question: would any of these interpretations of life as either totally bereft of meaning or dignity, or wholly negative, or purely accidental, reconcile us to living? Is not an indwelling and immortal vision of the ideal, however fragmentary and incommunicable, the only and the eternally propulsive mood of the spirit? The great positive note of the poem is this: whatever accidents befall it in experience, humiliation is a casualty to which the human spirit is never subject.

The poem is too long for quotation in its entirety, but the opening figure is a picture of such rare and haunting beauty that quotation seems inevitable:

71

"Between me and the sunset, like a dome
Against the glory of a world on fire,
Now burned a sudden hill,
Bleak, round, and high, by flame-lit height
    made higher,
With nothing on it for the flame to kill
Save one who moved and was alone up there
To loom before the chaos and the glare
As if he were the last god going home
Unto his last desire.

Dark, marvellous, and inscrutable he moved on
Till down the fiery distance he was gone,
Like one of those eternal, remote things
That range across a man's imaginings
When a sure music fills him and he knows
What he may say thereafter to few men,—
The touch of ages having wrought
An echo and a glimpse of what he thought
A phantom or a legend until then;
For whether lighted over ways that save,
Or lured from all repose,
If he go on too far to find a grave,
Mostly alone he goes."

And, since they contain the final essence of what the
poet has to say of the meaning of life, we may well
quote the closing lines of the poem; the eternal question which the spirit sends rocketing into the far, un-
charted corners of the universe:

"If after all that we have lived and thought,
    All comes to Nought,—
    If there be nothing after Now,
    And we be nothing anyhow,

E. A. ROBINSON

And we know that,—why live?
'Twere sure but weaklings' vain distress
To suffer dungeons where so many doors
Will open on the cold eternal shores
That look sheer down
To the dark tideless floods of Nothingness
Where all who know may drown."

VI: POSTSCRIPT

VI

POSTSCRIPT

It is comparatively simple for the critic, writing after the event and taking the long view, to discern in the publication of Mr. Robinson's first slim volume back in 1896 the most important event in American poetry since the close of Walt Whitman's career. This discovery, it may be recalled, was not made at the time. It was not until 1905, eight years after the first issue of *The Children of the Night,* that Theodore Roosevelt, then President of the United States, when reviewing that volume in *The Outlook,* called attention to the undoubted touch of genius which marked it and spoke of it as indicating the end of that "twilight of the poets" which had been so very grey in America. Surely not the least notable attributes of Mr. Robinson's poetic activity are the dignity and integrity of his attitude toward his art. Lack of recognition never caused him to compromise his ideals; long delayed recognition, when it came, found him still true to his own finest vision, still revealing without comment or explanation the inner light of his spirit.

His importance in our literature is hardly likely to be overestimated even by critics who are his contemporaries and who have therefore felt directly the

beauty and power of his art. He stands with Whitman among those few poets to whom no aspect of
human experience is insignificant, to whom no subject
in human life lies outside the field of art. He is certainly the most thoughtful of our poets and the most
responsive to intellectual experience. Beneath the im-
mediate emotional effect of his poems is the spell of
an intellectual magic unique in American poetry. But
it is his consistent preoccupation with the effects of
life upon the mind and heart of man, his insight into
the central interests of life itself, his capacity for
revealing the spiritual possibilities of even the most
meagre contacts with actuality which constitute the
explicit distinction of his poetry.

The effect of his art upon his contemporaries has
been remarkable both for its intensity and its per-
vasiveness. It is certainly true that his poetry has
had a tremendous influence upon a whole generation
of American poets, that it has taught them not only
to see the true countenance of American life, but to
care deeply about it, to find in it the noblest material
for their use. It is not claiming too much to assert
that the more reflective and conscientious of our contemporary novelists have been peculiarly susceptible
to his influence and that to it has been due much of
the honesty and the courage that have found their
way into the record which these novelists are making
of our life. Not the least of Mr. Robinson's contributions to our literature has been the effect which he has
exercised upon other writers. And for this his own
sonnet in praise of George Crabbe phrases perfectly
the measure of our indebtedness:

E. A. ROBINSON

"Whether or not we read him, we can feel
From time to time the vigor of his name
Against us like a finger for the shame
And emptiness of what our souls reveal
In books that are as altars where we kneel
To consecrate the flicker, not the flame."

BIBLIOGRAPHY
OF THE WRITINGS OF
EDWIN ARLINGTON ROBINSON
By
W. VAN R. WHITALL

THE TORRENT AND THE NIGHT BEFORE

1896

THE TORRENT/AND THE NIGHT BEFORE/
BY EDWIN ARLINGTON/ROBINSON, GARDI-
NER/MAINE, 1889-1896/ *Qui pourrais-je imiter
pour être original?*/Coppée/PRINTED FOR THE
AUTHOR/MDCCCXCVI/

> COLLATION: Title page as above, verso, Copy-
> right, 1896,/By Edwin Arlington Robinson./
> The Riverside Press, Cambridge, Mass.,
> U. S. A./Printed by H. O. Houghton and Com-
> pany./; Dedication, page three: "This book is
> dedicated to any man,/woman, or critic who
> will cut the/edges of it. I have done the top."/
> Verso, Blank. Text, pp. 5-44. Duodecimo
> 6¾ x 4¼.

Issued in blue paper covers, bearing the title on front
cover: "The Torrent &/The Night Before/"
First issue of First Book.

THE POETRY OF

THE CHILDREN OF THE NIGHT

1897

The Children of the Night/A Book of Poems/By/
EDWIN ARLINGTON ROBINSON/ (Ornament)/
Boston/Richard G. Badger & Company/MDCCCXCVII/

> COLLATION: Four unnumbered pages, the fourth
> containing the following declaration: "This first
> edition of The Children of the Night con-/sists
> of Five Hundred Copies on Batchworth Laid/
> Paper, and Fifty Copies on Imperial Japanese
> Vellum/Richard G. Badger & Company"/.
> Half Title, page I: The Children of the Night/,
> verso blank. Title as above, page III, verso,
> Copyright, 1896 and 1897,/by Edwin Arlington
> Robin-/son. All rights reserved./
> The cover design is by/Mr. T. B. Hapgood, Jr./
> Dedication page V: "To the Memory/of/My
> Father and Mother"/, Verso, blank. Contents
> pp. VII, VIII and IX, verso blank, and Text
> pp. 11-121. Page 122 blank while 123 con-
> tains imprint: "Printed by John Wilson and
> Son/at the University Press, Cam/bridge, for
> Richard G. Badger/and Company, Publishers,
> Boston/, verso, blank. Duodecimo 6¾ x 4¼.

Issued in muslin covered boards. Decorations
green and red. Front and back covers lettered in

E. A. ROBINSON

green, "THE CHILDREN/OF THE NIGHT"/ Edwin Arlington Robinson/
Lettered and decorated on back in green.
Lettering "THE CHIL-/DREN/OF THE/NIGHT."/
Robinson/Badger/
Edges untrimmed.
First Edition.   First issue.

THE POETRY OF

Limited Edition of

THE CHILDREN OF THE NIGHT

1897

The Children of the Night/A Book of Poems/by/
EDWIN ARLINGTON ROBINSON/ (ornament)
BOSTON/RICHARD G. BADGER & COMPANY/
MDCCCXCVII/

> COLLATION: Four unnumbered pages, all blank
> except the fourth, which contains the declara-
> tion found on the fourth unnumbered page of
> the first issue. Pages I-X consisting of Half
> Title, Verso blank; Title as quoted, Verso
> Copyright and "The cover design is by/Mr.
> T. B. Hapgood, Jr./"; Dedication, page V,
> verso blank; Contents pages VII, VIII and
> IX, verso blank. Text pp. 11-121. Page 122
> blank, 123 containing printer's imprint and
> blank page 124. The eighth signature con-
> tains but six leaves. Duodecimo 6¾ x 4¼.
> All edges untrimmed.

Issued as a special edition consisting of fifty copies
printed on Imperial Japanese Vellum. Front and back
covers blank. Lettered on back: The/Children/of
the/Night/Robinson/Badger/1897/
First edition second issue limited.

E. A. ROBINSON

CAPTAIN CRAIG

1902

CAPTAIN CRAIG/A Book of Poems/By/Edwin
Arlington Robinson/(Printer's device.)/Boston and
New York/HOUGHTON, MIFFLIN & COMPANY/
The Riverside Press, Cambridge/1902/

> COLLATION: Duodecimo (7½ x 4⅞). Blank
> leaf. Title page as above, verso: "Copyright,
> 1902, by Edwin Arlington Robinson/All
> Rights Reserved/Published October, 1902/Of
> the first edition One Hundred and/twenty-five
> Copies have been printed and/bound entirely
> uncut with paper label"/. Contents page and
> verso blank. Text pp. 1-171. Printer's im-
> print: Verso of page 171, THE RIVERSIDE
> PRESS/Electrotyped and printed by H. O.
> Houghton & Co./Cambridge, Mass., U. S. A./

Issued in green linen covered boards with paper label
on back, lettered: Captain/Craig/A/Book of/Poems/
("A book of poems" in red). Robinson/First Edition/
(All other lettering, black, with a red line across the
top of "Captain" and across top of "First Edition").
This is the first issue of the first edition.

THE POETRY OF

CAPTAIN CRAIG

1902

CAPTAIN CRAIG/A Book of Poems/By/Edwin
Arlington Robinson/(Printer's device) /Boston and
New York/HOUGHTON, MIFFLIN & COMPANY/
The Riverside Press, Cambridge/1902/

> Second issue of First Edition. Has same col-
> lation as first issue, with exception that there
> is no declaration at bottom of verso of title
> page, has no paper label and is issued in cloth,
> with blind stamped lines around edges of front
> and back covers. Top edges gilt. Gilt letter-
> ing on back—CAPTAIN/CRAIG/A/BOOK/
> OF/POEMS/EDWIN/ARLINGTON/ROB-
> INSON/HOUGHTON/MIFFLIN/& CO./

E. A. ROBINSON

CAPTAIN CRAIG

1903

CAPTAIN CRAIG/A Book of Poems/By/Edwin Arlington Robinson/Second Edition/(Printer's Device) Boston and New York/HOUGHTON, MIFFLIN & COMPANY/The Riverside Press, Cambridge/1903/

> COLLATION: One blank leaf, title page as above, verso Copyright, 1902, by Edwin Arlington Robinson/All Rights Reserved/Published October, 1902/. Contents page, verso blank. Text pp. 1-171, with printer's imprint on verso of page 171: The Riverside Press/Electrotyped and printed by H. O. Houghton & Co./Cambridge, Mass., U. S. A./

Issued in light green cloth, top edges gilt; front and back covers blind stamped around edges; back, gilt line top and bottom with gilt lettering: CAPTAIN/CRAIG/A/BOOK OF/POEMS/EDWIN/ARLINGTON/ROBINSON/Houghton/Mifflin/& Co./Size: Duodecimo 7⅜ x 5. Second edition.

THE POETRY OF

THE CHILDREN OF THE NIGHT

1905

The Children of the Night/A Book of Poems/By/
EDWIN ARLINGTON ROBINSON/NEW YORK/
CHARLES SCRIBNER'S SONS/1905/

> COLLATION: Duodecimo (6⅞ x 4¼). Half
> title: The Children of the Night page I, verso
> blank. Title as above page III, verso, Copy-
> right, 1896 and 1897,/By Edwin Arlington
> Robin-/son. All rights reserved./Dedication:
> Page V, "To the Memory/of/My Father and
> Mother"/verso blank. Contents: pp. VII-IX,
> verso blank. Text pp. 11-121, verso, printer's
> imprint.

Issued in green silk covered boards, back lettered
"The/Chil/dren/of the/Night/Robinson/CSS/Front
cover contains title "THE CHILDREN/OF THE
NIGHT"/Edwin Arlington Robinson/within a ruled
border. All lettering and ruling done in gilt. All
edges uncut.
Second edition.

90

E. A. ROBINSON

THE TOWN DOWN THE RIVER

1910

THE TOWN DOWN/THE RIVER/A Book of Poems/By/Edwin Arlington Robinson/NEW YORK/ CHARLES SCRIBNER'S SONS/1910/

COLLATION: Duodecimo (6¾ x 4½) Eight pages consisting of: Half title, The Town Down the River/, verso, blank. Title, as above, verso, Copyright, 1910, by/CHARLES SCRIBNER'S SONS/Published September, 1910/Printer's device. Dedication: "To/ THEODORE ROOSEVELT"/. Verso blank. Contents leaf. Text 1-129.

Issued in green silk covered boards, gilt ruling on front cover, gilt lettering front cover: THE .TOWN/ DOWN .THE .RIVER/Edwin Arlington Robinson/. Back, gilt lettered: THE/TOWN/DOWN/THE/ RIVER/ROBINSON/CSS/. Top edges gilt, other edges untrimmed. First Edition.

THE POETRY OF

1914

VAN ZORN/A COMEDY IN THREE ACTS/By/
Edwin Arlington Robinson/New York/THE MAC-
MILLAN COMPANY/1914/All Rights Reserved/

> COLLATION: Octavo (7⁹⁄₁₆ x 5³⁄₁₆) consisting of
> five leaves as follows: Half title, verso printer's
> imprint. Title as above, verso, Copyright,
> 1914/By THE MACMILLAN COMPANY/
> Set up and electrotyped. Published Septem-
> ber, 1914/Copyright in Great Britain,/All act-
> ing rights reserved by the author/. Dedication
> "To/HERMANN HAGEDORN"/, verso
> blank. Half title, verso blank. Characters,
> verso blank. AND text pp. 1-164 and four
> leaves of publisher's advertisements.

Issued in dark maroon, with top and bottom edges
cut. The following title is stamped in gold across the
front cover and inclosed within rectangular gold lines:
VAN ZORN/A COMEDY IN THREE ACTS/Edwin
Arlington Robinson/. Gold lines across the top and
bottom of the back. Lettered in gold across the back:
Van/Zorn/Robinson/Macmillan/

E. A. ROBINSON

THE PORCUPINE

1915

THE PORCUPINE/A DRAMA IN THREE ACTS/
BY/EDWIN ARLINGTON ROBINSON/New York/
THE MACMILLAN COMPANY/1915/All rights re-
served/

COLLATION: Octavo four leaves and pp. 160;
consisting of, Half-title (with advertisement of
works by the same author upon the reverse);
Title-page, as above, with copyright on reverse;
Dedication page, verso blank; Half title, verso
blank, and page one, containing list of CHAR-
ACTERS, verso blank, with ERRATUM slip
added. Pages 3-152 text and four leaves publisher's advertisements. There is no printer's
imprint; no signatures.

Issued in dark maroon, top gilt and fore-edges trimmed.
Front cover contains title, THE PORCUPINE/
EDWIN ARLINGTON ROBINSON/in gilt letters,
within gilt rectangular lines. Gilt lines across the top
and bottom of the back, and lettered in gold across
the back: THE/PORCUPINE/ROBINSON/MAC-
MILLAN/
Size of sheets, 7⅛ x 4⅞. First edition.

93

THE POETRY OF

NOTE: The declaration on copyright page states the publication simultaneously in the United States and Great Britain. Also, the list of books on verso of Half-title page contains the Title, "Flammonde," as in preparation.

E. A. ROBINSON

CAPTAIN CRAIG

1915

CAPTAIN CRAIG/A Book of Poems/By/EDWIN
ARLINGTON ROBINSON/REVISED EDITION/
WITH ADDITIONAL POEMS/New York/THE
MACMILLAN COMPANY/1915/. All rights re-
served/

> COLLATION: Duodecimo ($7\frac{5}{16}$ x $4\frac{7}{8}$). Page
> containing half title: CAPTAIN CRAIG/verso
> Printer's imprint. Title page as above, verso:
> Copyright, 1902 and 1915, by Edwin Arlington
> Robinson/All rights reserved/Published Octo-
> ber, 1902/Revised Edition February, 1915/
> (Note: Previous issues of this title have no
> dedication). Dedication page: To/THE
> MEMORY OF/JOHN HAYS GARDI-
> NER/verso, blank. Contents page, verso
> blank. Text pp. 1-182. Page 183 contains
> the announcement within rectangular ruling, in
> the centre of the page: The following pages
> contain advertisements of/books by the same
> author or on kindred subjects/Then follows one
> blank page and five pages of advertisements.

Issued in dark red cloth, front cover blind stamped
around the edges, with blind stamped title: CAPTAIN

THE POETRY OF

CRAIG/A BOOK OF POEMS/(Line)/EDWIN AR-
LINGTON ROBINSON/Gilt lines top and bottom of
back, gilt lettered: CAPTAIN/CRAIG/A BOOK/OF
POEMS / ROBINSON / MACMILLAN / All edges
trimmed. Other editions conclude with the poem
"Twilight Song" page 169, while this closes with "The
Field of Glory." First issue of the Revised Edition.

E. A. ROBINSON

THE MAN AGAINST THE SKY

1916

THE MAN AGAINST THE SKY/A Book of Poems/
By/Edwin Arlington Robinson/New York/The Macmillan Company/1916/All rights reserved/

COLLATION: pp. XII-149 consisting of half title,
verso, advertisement of author's books, I-II;
Title as above, verso copyright and printer's
imprint, III-IV; Dedication, verso blank, V-
VI; Acknowledgements, verso blank, VII-VIII;
Contents, IX-X; Half title, verso blank, XI-
XII. Text p. 1-149. Verso of 149 blank. An-
nouncement of publisher's advertisements p.
151, verso blank, then four pages of publisher's
advertisements. Duodecimo (6¾ x 4½).

Issued in dark red cloth, t.e.g. Gilt lettered title and
author's name front cover; back gilt lettered title and
author's name.

97

THE POETRY OF

THE PETERBOROUGH IDEA

1916

THE "NORTH AMERICAN REVIEW" for September 1916 contains the following: "THE PETERBOROUGH IDEA/By Edwin Arlington Robinson"/. AND REPRINTED BY PERMISSION, FROM THE "NORTH AMERICAN REVIEW" in pamphlet, size 7 x 6, on white paper bearing the water mark "Alexandra," by the MacDowell Memorial Association, Peterborough, N. H., 1917.

E. A. ROBINSON

MERLIN

1917

MERLIN/A Poem/By/Edwin Arlington Robinson/
New York/THE MACMILLAN COMPANY/
1917/All rights reserved/

> COLLATION: Three unnumbered leaves and 168
> pp. text, consisting of half title, verso adver-
> tisement of books by the same author; Title as
> above, verso copyright and printer's imprint;
> Dedication, verso blank; Text pp. 1-168; p.
> 169 contains announcement of author's books
> by the publisher, verso blank, then four pp.
> advertisements.

Issued as duodecimo, with leaves 6½ x 4½, in red
cloth boards, gilt lettered front and back. Top and
bottom edges cut.

99

THE POETRY OF

THE CHILDREN OF THE NIGHT

1919

The Children of the Night./A Book of Poems/By/
Edwin Arlington Robinson/NEW YORK/CHARLES
·SCRIBNER'S SONS/1919/

> COLLATION: Pages I-X and Text 11-121; Half
> Title, verso blank; Title as above, verso copy-
> right and printer's imprint; Dedication, blank
> verso; Contents VII-IX; page X blank. The
> verso of p. 121 is blank. Size reduced to
> 6¾ x 4¼. Top edges trimmed, others uncut.

Issued in green cloth covered boards, lettered on front
cover and back, in gilt same as second edition.
Third edition.

E. A. ROBINSON

THE THREE TAVERNS

1920

THE THREE TAVERNS/A BOOK OF POEMS/
BY/EDWIN ARLINGTON ROBINSON/Author of
"The Man Against the Sky,"/ "Merlin, A Poem,"
etc./New York/THE MACMILLAN COMPANY/
1920/All rights reserved/Issued in maroon cloth covered boards 6¾ x 4¾, gilt lettered on back only.

COLLATION: Ten unnumbered pages and 120
pages text, as follows: Half title, verso publisher's imprint; blank, verso list of author's
books; Title as above, verso copyright; Dedication, verso blank; Contents, verso contents and
acknowledgements; text pp. 1-120. All edges
trimmed.

101

THE POETRY OF

THE TOWN DOWN THE RIVER

1920

THE TOWN DOWN/THE RIVER/A Book of
Poems/BY/EDWIN ARLINGTON ROBINSON/
NEW YORK/CHARLES SCRIBNER'S SONS/
1920/

> Has same collation as first edition, but issued
> with trimmed edges and in dark green cloth
> boards.

Second Edition.

E. A. ROBINSON

LANCELOT

1920

LANCELOT/A Poem/BY/EDWIN ARLINGTON
ROBINSON/(Device)/New York/THOMAS SELT-
ZER/1920/
Special edition of 450 copies for the/LYRIC SO-
CIETY/New York/

> COLLATION: Three leaves as follows: Half title,
> verso list of author's books; Title, verso copy-
> right; Dedication, verso blank and 184 pages
> text.

Issued in dark maroon, edges trimmed, gilt lettered
title front cover, and back.
Limited Edition.

THE POETRY OF

1920

LANCELOT/A Poem/By/EDWIN ARLINGTON ROBINSON/(Device) New York/THOMAS SELTZER/1920/ Issued in green-grey cloth covered boards, with sheets 6⅝ x 4½; edges cut. Front cover, and back gilt lettered.

> COLLATION: Six unnumbered pages and 184 pp. text; half title, verso list of author's books; Title as above, verso copyright; Dedication, verso blank. (There is a limited edition of this printing.)

First Edition.

E. A. ROBINSON

AVON'S HARVEST

1921

AVON'S HARVEST/By/EDWIN ARLINGTON
ROBINSON/New York/THE MACMILLAN COM-
PANY/1921/All rights reserved/

> COLLATION: Six unnumbered pages consisting
> of, half title, list of author's works, title, Copy-
> right, dedication, blank and 65 pp. text.

Issued in light maroon boards with dark maroon cloth
back gilt lettered, and paper label on front cover.
Octavo with sheets 8⅛ x 5⅜.

105

THE POETRY OF

COLLECTED POEMS

1921

COLLECTED POEMS/By/EDWIN ARLINGTON
ROBINSON/New York/THE MACMILLAN COM-
PANY/1921/All rights reserved/

> COLLATION: XII pages as follows: Half title,
> verso, publisher's imprint; Title as above, verso,
> Copyright and "Printed in the United States of
> America" at top of page; Acknowledgments,
> verso blank; Contents VII-XI, verso blank
> and Text pp. 1-592, text ending on page 591.
> Facing the title is a portrait of the author from
> a painting by Lilla Cabot Perry, painted in
> 1916.

Issued in blue cloth covered boards, measuring
8 x 5½; gilt lettered on back: "COLLECTED/
POEMS"/. ROBINSON/MACMILLAN/. All edges
trimmed. Stamped line around edges front cover.
First issue of First Edition.
Reprinted 1922 with minor corrections.

E. A. ROBINSON

LIMITED COLLECTED EDITION, TWO VOLUMES

1921

VOLUME I.

COLLATION: Six unnumbered pages as follows: Half title, "Collected Poems"/Vol. I/; verso, blank; Statement as to number printed, "This special edition is published by/The Brick Row Book Shop, Inc./through the courtesy of/The Macmillan Company, and is/limited to two hundred copies,/numbered and signed by the author,/of which this is ———/————/" verso blank; Title page, "The Collected Poems/of/EDWIN ARLINGTON/ROBINSON/IN TWO VOLUMES/VOL. I/The BRICK ROW BOOK SHOP, Inc./New Haven, NEW YORK, Princeton/1921," verso, Copyright, and 314 pages text, beginning with "The Man Against the Sky." Facing Title Page is a silver point drawing of the author by Bradford Perin.

VOLUME II.

COLLATION: Four unnumbered pages as follows: Half title, "Collected Poems/Vol. II/," verso blank; Title Page like Volume I, but for "Vol. II," verso, Copyright, and text pp. 315-591. This volume begins with the poem· "The Master," on page 317.

THE POETRY OF

THERE IS NO INDEX. Size of covers same as the First Edition of Collected Poems.

Issued in blue paper covered boards, with paper label, lettered: "Collected Poems/of/EDWIN/ARLINGTON/ROBINSON/The Brick Row/Book Shop, Inc./," on the back for "Vol. I" and "Vol. II." Heavy linen backs. A list of the subscribers is laid in with the following title, "SUBSCRIBERS/to the/ Limited Collected Edition/of the Poems of/EDWIN ARLINGTON/ROBINSON/PUBLISHED BY/The BRICK ROW BOOK SHOP, Inc./1921/." Gilt tops, other edges uncut.

E. A. ROBINSON

1921

THE YEAR BOOK OF THE POETRY SOCIETY
OF SOUTH CAROLINA, for 1921, contains the following from the pen of Edwin Arlington Robinson:
"Peterborough, N. H.,/September 15, 1921./Please
let me write a few words as one who is/greatly inter-
ested in the Poetry Society of South/Carolina, and
as one who believes that its existence/is significant not
only to the South, but to the North/and the East and
the West. Many poems that have/been written by
contemporary Southern authors are/of a quality to
make us up here in the North wish/that a few Pal-
mettoes might be persuaded to sprout/and spread
themselves along with our native pines/and hemlocks
which are [not] always murmuring."

THE POETRY OF

AVENEL GRAY

1922

POETRY—A Magazine of Verse/, Edited by Harriet
Monroe/Tenth Birthday Number/October 1922/
CONTAINS POEM BY EDWIN ARLINGTON
ROBINSON ENTITLED "Avenel Gray," found on
pages 1-14.

E. A. ROBINSON

ENGLISH COLLECTED EDITION

1922

COLLECTED POEMS/By/EDWIN ARLINGTON ROB-
INSON/With an Introduction by/JOHN DRINKWATER/
(Device)
London/CECIL PALMER/OAKLEY HOUSE, 14
BLOOMSBURY STREET/W.C.I./

> COLLATION: Twenty-two pages as follows:
> Half title, reverse side blank; Title as above,
> verso copyright; Acknowledgments, verso
> blank; Introduction pp. VII-XVI; Contents
> pp. XVII-XXII. Text pp. 1-591. Facing title
> page is portrait by Lilla Cabot Perry from
> painting made in 1916.

Issued in half brown cloth with imitation leather back.
Title in gilt, on back. Top edges cut, others untrimmed.

THE POETRY OF

THE FOLLOWING BOOKS CONTAIN POEMS BY
MR. ROBINSON NOT PUBLISHED ELSEWHERE

1918

The Masque of Poets, A Collection of New Poems
by Contemporary American Poets Edited by Edwin
J. O'Brien. New York, Dodd, Mead and Company,
1918.   Page 98, "Genevieve and Alexandra,/Edwin
Arlington Robinson"/beginning, "Genevieve"/
     "Don't look at me so much as if to-day
     Were the last day on earth for both of us!"
And ending "Genevieve"/
     "Oh, stop that!"

1921

The Pilgrim Spirit, by George P. Baker. Boston, 1921.
"The Pilgrims' Chorus/By Edwin Arlington Robinson/
Music by Leo Sowerby"/Pages 77 and 78.

BIOGRAPHICAL NOTE

BIOGRAPHICAL NOTE

Edwin Arlington Robinson was born at Head Tide, Maine, on December 22, 1869, the son of Edward and Mary E. (Palmer) Robinson. In 1870 his parents removed from Head Tide to Gardiner, Maine, and Mr. Robinson received his early education there. After graduating from the Gardiner High School, he went to Harvard College, where he studied from 1891 to 1893. He spent the years of 1897 and 1898 in New York City, returning there in 1900. His first book of poems, *The Torrent and The Night Before,* a pamphlet privately printed and now exceedingly rare, was published in 1896. His second volume, the first offered to the general public, *The Children of the Night,* was published in 1897.

From 1900 on he resided in New York City, engaging in various occupations, but gave his time chiefly to the writing of poetry. During the years 1903-4 he was an inspector in the New York subway, then in course of construction. From 1905 to 1909 he did office work in the Custom House in New York through the friendly influence of President Roosevelt. He finally found that poetry required all his time, and, as he says, "somehow or other found a way to write it."

During the years from 1897 to 1922 there have been published eight volumes of poetry and two plays by

E. A. ROBINSON

Mr. Robinson, in addition to the *Collected Poems* which were issued in 1921. The complete bibliography included in this book makes enumeration of these volumes here unnecessary. A long dramatic poem entitled "Roman Bartholow" is announced for publication in the spring of 1923. When people ask Mr. Robinson for a rating of his own poems, he tells them to wait until he has been dead for at least fifty years. In a recent letter he has said: "I came to realise that a poet begins to live, if he lives at all, only after he is dead, and long ago ceased worrying about it."

Since 1911 much of his poetry has been composed at the MacDowell Colony, Petersborough, New Hampshire, where for eleven years Mr. Robinson has spent his summers, finding in that beautiful spot ideal conditions for uninterrupted creative activity.

In 1922 the Authors Club selected Mr. Robinson's *Collected Poems* as the most significant contribution to literature made by any American during the previous year; that choice was the occasion which called forth the present little essay. In the same year Mr. Robinson's volume received both the Pulitzer prize for poetry and that of the Poetry Society. Academic recognition came in an honorary degree of Litt. D. conferred by Yale University at the 1922 Commencement. Mr. Robinson is a member of the National Institute of Arts and Letters.

THE END

116